Awesome Warm and Cold Soups!

Delicious Soup Recipes for Everyone!

BY: Ivy Hope

Copyright/License Page

Table of Contents

Introduction

We literally can all remember at least one time in your life heard someone said to us: "Have a soup, you will feel better" or "let me bring you're a hot potage that will cheer you up." Does it mean that soups can miraculously heal our wounds, physical and mental? Well, we are not doctors; we are cooks, so we will not pronounce ourselves officially on that matter. However, let us just say that if eating a soup, sip on a cup of bouillon, then please do not ask yourself twice and start cooking.

Let us find out how long soups have actually been served! You may or may not actually be surprised to hear that they appeared before Jesus Christ and they were very basic. Over a fire or hot rocks, in clay pots, some vegetables, water, meat and herbs would be cooked for a while, and the first soups were born. Being used main meals at times, they become over the years appetizers or sides to a more complete meal.

Soups eventually appeared on almost every restaurant's menus. Each country or region offers some specialty soups. Miso soups are Japanese's specialties, Chinese egg drop soup, German potato soup, and so on. However, there is indeed nothing like making your own soup based on the ingredients you simply love. Put the soup you love on your menu any day. Make a soup is a warm thick hearty soup on a cold winter day for the family.

So, let us finish this introduction and line up the main ingredients or staples you should always keep in your pantry and/or refrigerator. First, always keep some type of broth. I would suggest at least having vegetable broth, but it's better if you do also keep chicken and beef broth so you can really perfect some soups. Also, if you are using the broth after cooking your beef or chicken, then keep it safely in the freezer until ready to use it. Secondly, always keep plenty of dried herbs and spices. For soups, you will often use oregano, thyme, basil, sage, rosemary, garlic power and onion powder, salt pepper, cumin and more. If you planted fines herbs in the garden, use them up and use some fresh garlic and onion as well if you can.

In your pantry, you will always want to store some tomato paste, tomato sauce and diced tomatoes, just in case. Also, keep some cornstarch in case you need to thicken the soup. Moreover, make sure to stock up in soya sauce, hot sauce, Worchestire sauce and also some uncooked rice and small noodles if you decide to add some starchy ingredients to your soups.

In addition, it may not be a bad idea to keep some frozen vegetables in case of an emergency soup situation; if not, I surely recommend making your soups with fresh veggies instead.

Spicy cold tomato soup

We are starting this book with a bang, and it is a spicy one! This soup will give your taste buds something to talk about with your friends. Moreover, it will literally give you a very good option to a simple tomato juice or even Bloody Mary. Let us do this!

Serving Size: 2

Cooking Time: 30 Minutes

Ingredients:

- 3 large diced fresh tomatoes
- 1 tbsp. fresh minced basil
- 1/2 tbsp. fresh minced thyme
- 1 tbsp. Minced garlic
- ½ tbsp. onion powder
- 1 tbsp. Sirach sauce
- Black pepper
- 1 tbsp. olive oil
- 3 cups vegetable broth.
- Garlic croutons when serving

Instructions:

1. First, in your large pot, heat the olive oil and cook the garlic and fine herbs for 5 minutes.

2. Meanwhile, cut up the three tomatoes and set aside.

3. In the pot, add the broth, tomatoes, spices and sauce.

4. Let all the ingredients simmer on low temperature for about 20 minutes.

5. We will cook the soup but eat it cold. We let the ingredients simmer together to make sure all flavors combine well. So, after the soup has cooled down, place in the blender.

6. You will most likely have to proceed in two bathes. Activate the blender and blend until the consistency is completely smooth.

7. Serve when ready with a few croutons on top.

8. Keep the leftovers in the refrigerator.

Special vegetables soup

What makes this soup special? Come on, every soup in this book is special! That's the correct answer! However, specifically in this case, the vegetables we choose for you marry so well together with the herbs chosen as well.

Serving Size: 4

Cooking Time: 45 Minutes

Ingredients:

- 3 cups chopped fresh kale
- 1 large sliced carrot
- 1 large sliced zucchini
- 1 small can of diced tomatoes
- ½ chopped yellow onion
- 1 tbsp. minced garlic
- 1 large peeled and diced white potato
- ½ tsp. dried oregano
- ½ tsp. dried rosemary
- Salt, black pepper
- 1 tbsp. olive oil
- 5-6 cups turkey or chicken broth

Instructions:

1. Prepare all the vegetables. Chop and set aside.

2. Heat some oil in a large saucepan.

3. Add the garlic, onion and sliced zucchini and cook for a few minutes.

4. Add next broth and the sliced carrot and potato. Bring the soup to boil, then cook for about 10 minutes on high temperature to make sure the veggies get tender.

5. Reduce next to simmering; add the diced tomatoes, kale, herbs and spices.

6. Continue cooking for another 20-25 minutes.

7. I sometimes decide to add some cooked rice to the soup, so keep it as an option.

8. Enjoy this warm healthy soup any day of the week.

Roasted potatoes, bacon and herbs potage

Indeed, this is the perfect soup on a cold winter night. Add some meatballs or left over beef roast, and you are in for a complete meal. I love the savory combination of the fresh sage with potatoes and cooked bacon. Let us not forget some hearty bouillon you may have saved from your last chicken or turkey you baked.

Serving Size: 4

Cooking Time: 50-55 Minutes

Ingredients:

- 2 tbsp. all-purpose flour
- 4 cups turkey broth
- 4 cooked and crumbled all pork bacon
- 4 medium size red skin potatoes
- 1 tbsp. minced garlic
- ¼ cup diced red onion
- 1 tbsp. fresh minced sage
- 2 tbsp. fresh minced parsley
- ½ cup sour cream
- 1 cup heavy cream
- Salt, black pepper
- 1 tbsp. smoked paprika
- 1 tbsp. unsalted butter

Instructions:

1. Clean and dice the red skin potatoes. You will then start heating on medium heat the butter in the large saucepan and cook red onion, garlic and herbs for 5 minutes.

2. Add the potatoes and cook for another 10-12 minutes.

3. Meanwhile, cook the bacon and remove all excess grease after it is done.

4. Then, add the broth to the saucepan, along with the spices and herbs. Add the flour and bring to boil until you can see that the soup consistency has thicken. You should stir often so nothing sticks.

5. Continue cooking on low temperature for another 25-30 minutes. Add slowly the cream and the sour cream.

6. You will add the crumble cooked bacon as topping on the soup when serving.

7. In addition, you can keep a little minced fresh sage as decoration.

Cold cucumber and dill cream

This soup reminds me slightly of some dipping sauce I tasted in the past at the Greek restaurant. However, I like to think that this creation is quite unique, because not only it is served cold, but it is also served with fresh dill and chopped red onions.

Serving Size: 2

Cooking Time: 30 Minutes

Ingredients:

- 1 large seedless cucumber
- 1 cup plain Greek yoghurt
- 1 tbsp. fresh minced dill
- 1 tbsp. fresh minced parsley
- ½ tsp. onion powder
- ½ tsp. garlic powder
- Salt, pepper
- ½ tsp. lemon juice
- 2 cups vegetables broth

Instructions:

1. There will be no cooking in this recipe. No heat.

2. Dice the cucumber and mince the dill and the parsley first.

3. Next, place half of the ingredients in the blender container and activate.

4. Pour the cold soup into a large bowl and continue adding in the blender the other half.

5. Make sure the consistency is exactly how you like it.

6. Also, verify the spices by tasting the mixture before serving.

7. Decorate with a few slices of cucumbers and/or parsley leaves.

Delightful cream of carrots

This beautiful orange potage will be created in hardly no time! Make sure you do use fresh carrots, do not settle for canned or frozen ones. If you have a garden, please go pick up carrots from the garden and chop them up to create this amazing soup!

Serving Size: 3-4

Cooking Time: 45 Minutes

Ingredients:

- 1 tbsp. cornstarch
- 2 large sliced carrots
- 1 medium peeled and diced sweet potato
- 4 cups turkey broth
- 1 cup 10 % cream
- ½ tsp. white pepper and salt
- ½ tsp. ground cumin
- 1 tbsp. unsalted butter
- Pinch cinnamon

Instructions:

1. First, start by peeling and slicing the carrots and sweet potato.

2. Boil some water in a medium saucepan and cook for 12-15 minutes the root veggies until soft. Remove the excess water and set aside.

3. Rinse the saucepan and use it again. Heat the butter and add the cornstarch.

4. Add the broth, spices and herbs and bring to a boil for about 5 minutes, while stirring.

5. In the blender, place half of the veggies, broth and cream. Activate and pour back into the saucepan.

6. Then, repeat the same action for the rest of the ingredients and pour all together.

7. Keep warm until ready to serve and place some pita chips on the table.

Spaghetti sauce like soup

I noticed my son would also decline to eat soup when he was little. He thought soups were for grown-ups or they were too hot or too spicy. I had a few tricks in my sleeve. I started placing some of his favorite dishes in bowls instead of plates, and soon enough, I created this version of this spaghetti sauce soup, and he still loves it until this day!

Serving Size: 2

Cooking Time: 60 Minutes

Ingredients:

- 1 pound lean ground meat
- 1 diced green bell pepper
- 1 large can of crushed tomatoes
- 1 tbsp. minced garlic
- 2 tbsp. Tomato paste
- 2 cups tomato juice
- 1 cup vegetables broth
- 1 Tbsp. dried Italian seasonings
- Salt, black pepper
- Pinch red pepper flakes
- Some olive oil

Instructions:

1. First, in a large skillet, heat some olive oil and cook some garlic and onion for 5 minutes.

2. Add the ground beef and continue cooking. Keep stirring with wooden spoon, so the meat stays crumbly.

3. Once the meat is cooked, remove excess fat, and set aside.

4. In a large saucepan, add the broth, tomatoes sauce, and juice and crushed tomatoes, along with the herbs and spices.

5. Finally, also add the meat and the veggies to the mix and let the future soup simmer for 30 minutes so the flavors mix perfectly.

6. Serve with slices of fresh bread.

Broccoli and very cheesy soup

Cream of broccoli and cheese is often offered on menus. If you are tired of being left with unsatisfied after tasting the ones made for you. Go ahead and follow this awesome recipe; you will be very pleased. Do not forget to add a pinch of love when making it!

Serving Size: 2

Cooking Time: 30 Minutes

Ingredients:

- 1 tbsp. unsalted butter
- 1 tbsp. cornstarch
- 1 cup shredded Cheddar cheese
- ½ cup shredded Mozzarella cheese
- 3 cups fresh chopped broccoli florets
- 3 cups turkey or chicken broth
- 2 cups whole milk
- Salt, black pepper
- 1 tbsp. minced fresh thyme
- ½ tsp. ground cumin

Instructions:

1. Prepare all the ingredients, set them ready on the counter.

2. Steam cook the broccoli first, either in the microwave or on the stovetop as you wish.

3. Next, in your large saucepan, heat the butter and add the cornstarch, on medium low temperature. Stir constantly and add slowly the broth, cheeses and cream. Keep temperature low and add the cooked broccolis and all spices and herbs.

4. You need to taste before serving, as always, and will most likely have to adjust spices to makes sure the cheese I not overtaking the flavor of the soup.

Cold radish quite unique soup

This soup can be an inquire taste. Radishes are an inquire tastes. However, for any radish lovers, this soup is going to be a pleasant surprise. I think it is refreshing and it is certainly beautiful to serve any guests you want to impress.

Serving Size: 4

Cooking Time: 40 Minutes

Ingredients:

- 2 cups sliced fresh radish
- 2 minced green onions
- 1 cup sour cream
- 2 large peeled diced white potatoes
- 1 tbsp. minced fresh parsley
- Salt, black pepper
- Pinch chili powder

Instructions:

You should start by cook the potatoes. I choose to boil them; you could also microwave them if you are in a hurry. The important things is that they come out tender.

1. You will also need to cook the radish before blending into a delicious soup.

2. Next, heat a little oil in a small skillet and the radishes for 5-6 minutes, or until they turn, clear.

3. Then, it is time to blend!

4. I always like to try to separate the mixture into 2 portions so it's easier to blend, and your machine does not get overworked.

5. Blend until the consistency is perfectly smooth. Taste and adjust the seasonings too as needed.

6. Pour into 4 bowls and decorate with green onions. Serve cold.

Mexican awesome meal soup

We will use fresh tomatoes, red beans, corn, and a few other special ingredients I will let you discover in the next minutes. We will also suggest topping it off with shredded sharp Cheddar cheese and crumbled corn chips. Ready?

Serving Size: 2

Cooking Time: 35-40 Minutes

Ingredients:

- 1 medium can crushed tomatoes
- 1 tsp. lime juice
- 1 tsp. minced fresh cilantro
- 1 tsp. minced garlic
- 1/2 cup corn kernel
- 1 cup red kidney beans, nicely rinsed and drained
- 1 cup vegetables broth
- 1 tsp. chili powder
- ½ tsp. onion powder
- Salt, black pepper
- ½ cups sharp shredded Cheddar cheese
- Handful corn chips
- Olive oil

Instructions:

1. In a medium saucepan, heat olive oil and lime juice on medium heat, cook the garlic and cilantro for a few minutes.

2. Add the corn, the red beans, the tomatoes and broth, as well as the spices and herbs.

3. Next, let all the ingredients cook together for about 30 minutes or so.

4. Taste and adjust the seasonings as needed.

5. Top each bowl with melted cheese and crumbled corn chips if you like.

French onion soup on Beef bouillon

We have to include a French onion soup in this cookbook. It is such a novelty and it is such a fun recipe to make at home. Let me warn you, however, that it is not cheap on your budget to recreate a good version of French onion soup. Plan to make it for a special occasion if you must!

Serving Size: 4

Cooking Time: 60 Minutes

Ingredients:

- 1 tbsp. all-purpose flour
- 6 cups beef broth, if you have homemade one, it's even better
- ½ envelop French onion soup dried seasonings
- 1 small sliced yellow onion
- 1 small sliced sweet onion
- 1 small sliced red onion
- 1 tbsp. minced garlic
- 1 tbsp. Worchestire sauce
- Salt, black pepper
- 2 cups shredded Swiss cheese
- ½ sliced French baguette (rather thick slices)
- 2 tbsp. unsalted butter

Instructions:

1. Preheat the oven to 425°F.

2. In a large saucepan, start by heating on medium temperature the butter.

3. Add all the onions and garlic. Make sure your onions are sliced thin and cook for about 10-12 minutes.

4. Add the beef broth and all other ingredients, except the cheese and the bread.

5. Continue simmering the broth for about 20 minutes.

6. Using French onions soups small porcelain bowls, divide the broth equally in 4.

7. Add one of 2 thick slices of bread and add a generous layer of Swiss cheese on top of it all.

8. Place the 4 bowls, in the oven and cook for about 12-15 minutes, or until the cheese is perfectly melted.

9. Serve right away, warning everyone that it will be extra hot. Dig in!

Zucchini and parmesan cheese soup

I find zucchinis are easy to transform into a soup. They can be sautéed in the pan with garlic and herbs before added to the blender. In this recipe, I will suggest adding some Parmesan cheese to make them taste so much richer. Serve with a side of French baguette.

Serving Size: 4

Cooking Time: 30 Minutes

Ingredients:

- 2/3 cup shredded Parmesan cheese
- 2 large sliced zucchinis
- 1 tbsp. minced garlic
- 1 small chopped sweet onion
- 1 tbsp. dried Italian seasonings
- 2 tbsp., minced fresh parsley
- 2 cups whole milk
- 2 cups turkey broth
- Unsalted butter

Instructions:

1. Get all your veggies out and heat the butter in a large saucepan on stovetop.

2. Add the garlic, onion and sliced zucchinis and cook for 12-15 minutes or until the zucchinis have soften.

3. Once that happens, add the broth, herbs and spices and let t simmer for another 10-15 minutes or so.

4. Next, divide the mixture in half and add half of the milk into the blender, as well as half of the cheese.

5. Activate the blender until the consistency is perfectly smooth.

6. Repeat with the rest of the ingredients.

7. Pour all the smooth mixture into the saucepan again and keep it warm until ready to serve.

Lime, avocado and jalapenos soup

This is a Mexican style soup without screaming traditional Mexican style. Why? First, it does not involve tomatoes, or cilantro, but involves other marvelous ingredients that can marry well together to create the desired yummy Mexican kick.

Serving Size: 4

Cooking Time: 45 Minutes

Ingredients:

- 5 cups chicken broth
- 1 cup sour cream
- 2 cups cooked chicken
- 2-3 medium fresh sliced jalapenos
- 1 tbsp. minced garlic
- ½ cup diced red onion
- 1 large diced avocado
- 2 tbsp. minced parsley
- Salt, black pepper
- 1 tsp. smoked paprika
- Olive oil

Instructions:

1. Prepare the garlic, onion and jalapenos. Please be careful handling the peppers, wear gloves and wash your hands after.

2. In a large saucepan, heat the olive oil on medium heat and cook the garlic, onion and peppers and parsley for 15 minutes or so.

3. Add the broth, the spices and the herbs along with the sour cream.

4. Stir well and keep on low temperature to cook for another 20 minutes. Add the cooked chicken and cook some more.

5. Serve with diced avocados on top of each bowl of soups, and perhaps some tortilla chips on the side.

Spinach simple soup

Spinach is my son's very favorite hot veggie. He cannot stand eating them raw, which is a different story for a different time. Therefore, I thrive on creating a few new spinach recipes a year. Let me share this one, and I will tell you it also involves cheese so it will be fabulous.

Serving Size: 2

Cooking Time: 30 Minutes

Ingredients:

- 4 cups baby spinach fresh leaves
- 2 cups ricotta cheese
- 1 cup shredded Parmesan cheese
- 3 cups turkey broth
- 1 tbsp. minced garlic
- 1 cup chopped yellow onion
- 1 tsp. ground cumin
- Salt, black pepper
- Unsalted butter

Instructions:

1. First, in a large skillet, heat the butter and cook garlic, onion for about 10 minutes.

2. Add the spinach leaves and cook for 5 minutes or so. Drain any excess water or butter and put aside.

3. In the blender, once the veggies are cooled down, add half of them with half of the rest of the ingredients.

4. Activate, and pour back into a saucepan to keep warm.

5. Repeat and let the soup warm back up until ready to serve.

6. I suggest serving with garlic and cheese crouton or simply a tablespoon of shredded Parmesan cheese sprinkle on top.

Pumpkin and sour cream cold soup

A cold pumpkin soup is a genius. It can be presented to your kids as a soup, snack or even dessert if you add the right ingredients. The sour cream will definitely help to balance the flavors and thickness. However, we will add some fall flavors such as nutmeg and cinnamon. Stay tuned!

Serving Size: 2

Cooking Time: 30 Minutes

Ingredients:

- 1 large can pumpkin puree
- ½ cup chopped sweet onion
- 1 cup sour cream
- 3 cups turkey or chicken broth
- ½ tsp. ground nutmeg
- ½ tsp. ground cinnamon
- ½ tsp. ground turmeric
- Some unsalted butter
- Pinch salt
- Pinch red pepper flakes
- Minced parsley to decorate

Instructions:

1. In a small pan, heat butter and cook the sweet onion for 7-8 minutes.

2. In the blender container, combine half of all ingredients, including of the onions once they have cooled off. Leave the parsley out.

3. Activate the blender and blend until you are satisfied with the texture.

4. Let the soup cool down and possibly put in the fridge for about 30 minutes before serving. Make sure you taste again before serving.

5. Decorate with fresh minced parsley.

Garlic and cauliflower potage

This cauliflower soup is out of the ordinary. The secret to making it super tasty is to add enough garlic and the right spices. In addition, we will use cream instead of milk. If you are opposed to adding some thick cream, please go ahead with milk and cornstarch for the thickness instead. Let us start, shall we!

Serving Size: 4

Cooking Time: 40 Minutes

Ingredients:

- 3 cups skinny cream (10 or 10%)
- 2 tbsp. all-purpose flour
- 2 tbsp. unsalted butter
- 1 large fresh cauliflower florets
- 2 tbsp. minced garlic
- 1 small chopped white onion
- 1 tbsp. fresh minced sage
- ½ dried thyme
- ½ tsp. dried oregano
- Salt, black pepper

Instructions:

1. First, wash and cut the cauliflower in small florets. Steam cook it until its tender.

2. Meanwhile, in a small pan melt some butter and cook the garlic for a few minutes.

3. In a large saucepan, melt the rest if the butter, add the flour and make a roux, stirring constantly.

4. Add slowly the cream, the herbs and the spices, and cooked cauliflowers, and keep cooking on medium heat, stirring occasionally.

5. Now, I personally do not like to reduce it to a puree-cream in the blender, but you could if you prefer.

6. I serve just as it with perhaps some cracker black pepper on top.

Celery and fine herbs yummy potage

I insist on you selecting fresh herbs as opposed to dried ones for this recipe. It will make all the difference in the world. Celery is not the most flavorful vegetable, so you ended to make sure to add the correct fresh herbs and spices to change it form plain to irresistibly delicious.

Serving Size: 3-4

Cooking Time: 30 Minutes

Ingredients:

- olive oil
- 2 cups chopped celery
- 1 small chopped leek
- 1 small chopped sweet onion
- 1 tbsp. minced garlic
- 1 tsp. celery seeds
- 1 tbsp. Fresh thyme
- 1 tbsp. minced fresh parsley
- 2 cups vegetables broth
- 2 1/2 cups whole milk
- Salt, black pepper

Instructions:

1. You will want to heat the oil in a large saucepan first.

2. Add the garlic, onion, chopped celery, fresh herbs and leek.

3. Cook the veggies for about 10-12 minutes or until the celery has soften.

4. Then, add the broth, milk and all the spices.

5. Continue to cook the veggies and broths together for another 15 minutes.

6. Before serving, place the ingredients in the blender and activate until the texture is perfectly smooth.

7. Add some crumbled crackers on top and voila!

Curry chicken noodles soup

Because a chicken noodles soup is necessary when you are not feeling well, we want to give you an additional option here. You may want to get or serve a simple chicken noodles soup, but if you want to add a little kick, this recipe is perfect for you. The curry will actually help, in most cases, clear your respiratory system, as well as adding a delicious note to the soup!

Serving Size: 4

Cooking Time: 50 Minutes

Ingredients:

- ½ bag uncooked egg noodles
- 2 cups cooked chicken
- 1 cup chopped carrot
- 1 cup chopped celery
- ¼ cup chopped yellow onion
- 1 tsp. garlic powder
- Salt, black pepper
- 2 tbsp. golden curry paste
- 6 cups chicken broth
- 1 tbsp. unsalted butter

Instructions:

1. In the largest saucepan, you have, heat some butter and cook the onion, celery and carrot for about 12-15 minutes.

2. Then, add about a cup of broth and the curry paste; use a whisk to make sure the paste dissolves well. Keep the heat to medium temperature.

3. Once the paste is all dissolved, it is time to add the rest of the broth and the other ingredients, except the cooked chicken. Bring to boil and add the noodles.

4. Cook the noodles until done, and then add the chicken to complete the recipe.

5. Adjust the seasonings and serve happily to your family.

Creamy sweet potatoes and mushrooms soup

Sweet potatoes are very healthy and yummy. When you decide to make a soup with them and sautéed mushrooms, you may find yourself in heaven on earth! The very earthy and savory flavors you will find in this potage will please you, and you can play with the herbs you prefer to add a little something special.

Serving Size: 4

Cooking Time: 50 Minutes

Ingredients:

- 1 tbsp. unsalted butter
- 1 tbsp. all-purpose flour
- 4 cups vegetable broth
- 2 cups light cream
- 1 tbsp. minced garlic
- 1/2 cup chopped yellow onion
- 1 small sliced peeled carrot
- 2 medium peeled sliced sweet potatoes
- 3 cups sliced button mushrooms
- Salt, black pepper
- 1 tsp. dried sage
- 1 tsp. ground cumin

Instructions:

1. First, in the microwave, cook the sweet potatoes for about 2-3 minutes each. I suggest cooking them whole and diced after. Do not overcook them at this time, they should not be mushy, just slightly soften.

2. In a large saucepan, heat the butter, and cook the garlic, mushrooms, carrots and onion for about 15 minutes.

3. Then, keep it on medium temperature. Add the rest of the butter, some flour and stir until to turns brownish, before adding the cream and continue stirring to get it thicken.

4. Finally add the broth and rest of spices and herbs. Stir to mix well and add the cooked diced potatoes.

5. Keep it on low temperature another 20 minutes until serving.

Very garlicky shrimp and noodles soup

This soup is very similar to a scampi style shrimp pasta dish, and that is on purpose. Why? Because it is delicious and so appreciated by everyone. I have no shame in making this lovely garlicky soup for my parents-in-law when they visit!

Serving Size: 2

Cooking Time: 40 Minutes

Ingredients:

- 1 /2 bag rice noodles
- ¼ pound medium deveined uncooked shrimp
- 1 tbsp. Minced garlic
- ½ tsp. garlic salt
- ½ tsp. onion powder
- 3 cups fish broth
- Some fresh minced parsley to decorate
- Some Unsalted butter

Instructions:

1. In a medium saucepan, sautéed the garlic in butter with the shrimp. Make sure the shrimp are cooked and pink before setting aside.

2. Add the broth and the spices and cook the rice noodles, it should take no more than about 6 minutes.

3. Add the cooked shrimp once the noodles are done and warm up all together before serving.

4. Place some shredded Parmesan on table to sprinkle on top of your excellent soups.

Dumplings and delicious turkey soup

Let us make some fresh dumplings, cook some veggies, and use our leftover turkey pieces. This will turn out perfect, I promise! I think this soup is even better if you are able to use the fresh turkey broth from the turkey you just baked, so this is the recipe to make the week after Thanksgiving.

Serving Size: 4

Cooking Time: 60 Minutes

For the dumplings:

- 1 cup all-purpose flour
- 1 tsp. baking powder
- Pinch salt
- ½ cup whole milk
- Butter

Soup:

- 6 cups turkey broth
- 1 large chopped carrot
- 2 chopped celery stalks
- 1 small chopped yellow onion
- 1 tbsp. minced garlic
- 2 ½ cups cooked turkey
- 1-2 bay leaves
- 1 tbsp. Italian seasonings
- Salt, black pepper

Instructions:

1. You should get 1 large saucepan out and a medium skillet.

2. In the saucepan, pour the broth and all seasonings and herbs.

3. Bring to boil.

4. Next, meanwhile, in a medium mixing bowl, combine the flour for the dumplings, add the salt, baking powder and add the milk and about 1 Tbsp. melted butter. Combine and mold the dumplings, you should have about 8-10.

5. Dump the flour dumplings one at a time in the boiling broth and cook for about 15-16 minutes.

6. Meanwhile, you are going to precook the veggies in the pan in butter: carrot, celery, garlic and onion.

7. When the dumplings are, done add the cooked turkey, cooked veggies and continue simmering the soup for about 10 minutes.

8. Taste and adjust seasonings. Then, remove the bay leaves.

9. Serve and smile.

Clam chowder with a kick

Nothing like a homemade clam chowder. I am being asked for the recipe each time I serve this very special soup to my guests and family. I have added a kick to it over the years, as my loved ones do thrive on spicy foods. Always remember you can tone down the spiciness as you wish.

Serving Size: 4

Cooking Time: 50 Minutes

Ingredients:

- 2 tbsp. unsalted butter
- 2 cans minced clams
- 2 large diced potatoes
- 1 small minced leek
- 1 small yellow onion
- 1 tbsp. minced garlic
- 1 tsp. white vinegar
- 3 cups half and half cream
- 1 cup vegetables broth
- Salt, black pepper
- 1 tsp. ground cumin

Instructions:

1. First, in a large saucepan, heat the butter and cook the garlic, onion and leek.

2. In a smaller saucepan, steam cook the potatoes. Drain well and set aside.

3. Add the clam juice, spices, herbs, vinegar and broth with the veggies.

4. Also slowly add the cream, the cooked potatoes and keep stirring, on medium temperature.

5. You will keep on cooking for 20-30 minutes and then finally add the clams for the last 10 cooking minutes. Taste and adjust the seasonings as needed.

6. Divide this delicious soup into 4 portions in bowls and serve with pita crackers.

Nice apple and curry soup

A soup made of apples is different. A soup made with curry and apples is very different but so lovable and tasty. We normally pair apples with cinnamon or nutmeg, but this time let us be real and create something new. We will add some curry paste, the red or golden one preferably. You will not be disappointed, I promise.

Serving Size: 2

Cooking Time: 30 Minutes

Ingredients:

- 2 medium red delicious apples, peeled and diced
- 1 tbsp. red curry
- 2 cups vegetables broth
- 1/2 cup sour cream
- 1 tbsp. agave syrup
- Pinch red pepper flakes
- Pinch salt

Instructions:

1. Let us be daring and let's make this awesome soup. Start by bringing to boil the broth and add the red curry paste. Stir in so it mixes well before adding the red apples and reduce the temperature to medium-low.

2. Next, cook for 15 minutes or until the apples have soften.

3. Add the red of the **Ingredients:** sour cream spices and diced apple in the broth.

4. Finally, when serving, add a swirl of agave syrup on top of the soup and just dig in.

Corn and sunflower seeds soup

If you are wondering where this unique combination of corns and sunflowers come from, let me tell you the story now. It was late summer one year ago, and we had organized a trip to cornfields to pick up our very own corns on the cob. We pick up bags of sunflowers seeds from the store as well snacking on them while cooking. From there, the leftovers led us to experiment and create this soup the very next day.

Serving Size: 4

Cooking Time: 45 Minutes

Ingredients:

- ¼ cup roasted sunflowers
- 2 cups kernel corn
- 3 cups turkey or chicken broth
- 1 cup chopped fresh kale
- ½ cup shredded Swiss cheese
- 1/3 cup sour cream
- ½ tsp. garlic salt
- ½ tsp. onion powder
- ½ tsp. red pepper flakes

Instructions:

1. I add kale to add color but if you do not like the bitterness, please replace it with bay spinach leaves instead.

2. You will fist bring to boil the broth with all spices and herbs.

3. Add the corn and the kale and mix well.

4. Lower the temperature and keep it on medium-low for the next 20 minutes.

5. Add the sour cream and cheese lastly, 10 minutes before serving. Bring up the temperature while stirring. Decorate the soup with plenty of sunflowers.

Superb white beans and veggies soup

This soup will be filled with beans and proteins for anyone who decides to eat it. It can totally be one of those meal soups. Double-up the recipe if you like and freeze individual portions in airtight containers to warm up during your busy week. In addition, if you want to top the soup with a layer of cheese, we will not tell anyone!

Serving Size: 4

Cooking Time: 35 Minutes

Ingredients:

- 1 small can crushed tomatoes
- 1 large can white kidney beans
- 2 cups fresh trimmed and cut green beans
- ½ cup diced red onion
- 1 tbsp. fresh minced cilantro
- 1 tbsp. Lemon juice
- 4 cups turkey or chicken broth
- Salt, black pepper
- 1 tsp. chili power
- Olive oil

Instructions:

1. Make sure you trim the fresh green beans well and cut them up in smaller pieces, and rinse and drain the beans.

2. Next, in a large saucepan, heat some olive oil and lemon juice and sautéed the garlic and onion, cilantro for 5 minutes.

3. Meanwhile, steam cook the trimmed green beans for 5 minutes just do they soften a little and drain them.

4. Add the green and white beans to the saucepan and the broth, crushed tomatoes, and additional seasonings to taste.

5. Keep it simmering for another 20 minutes and serve while it is hot.

White fish and turnip soup

You can choose your favorite white fish to use for this recipe. I suggest you pick tilapia or perhaps grouper, haddock, or even snapper. If you can be lucky, enough to use fresh fish if you are into fishing, then good for you, or ask your local fish market for a few good filets. Also, pick up a medium fresh turnip and let us cook!

Serving Size: 4

Cooking Time: 45 Minutes

Ingredients:

- 2 large cooked white fish
- 5 cups fish broth
- 1 tbsp., minced garlic
- 1 small chopped sweet onion
- 1 medium diced peeled turnip
- 2 tbsp. minced fresh parsley
- 1 tsp. celery seeds
- 1 tbsp. Italian seasonings
- Oliver oil
- 1 tsp. white pepper
- 1/2 tsp. sea salt

Instructions:

1. In a medium saucepan, boil the eater with salt and place the diced peeled turnip to boil. You want to cook them for about 15 minutes or until soften.

2. Meanwhile, in a larger saucepan, melt the oil and cook the garlic, onion and parsley for 5-6 minutes.

3. Add the broth and raise the temperature to medium high.

4. Add the cooked diced turnips next and cook another 15 minutes.

5. Finally, add all spices, the cooked pieces of fish and adjust the seasonings as needed before serving.

6. I usually place a lemon wedge on the side of the bowls when serving.

Conclusion

Well, here we are! We finished in beauty. We shared 25 yummy soup recipes that are all as delicious as a gun to make. Make it a family affair occasionally. Involve the children, cutting the veggies, measuring the broth, and picking up the fresh herbs from the garden.

In addition, I find soups are one of the best ways to let loose and start creating. Creating new recipes, adding some unusual ingredients is a great way to invent a brand new delightful soup. It is very important to cook soups slowly at low to medium temperatures. This way, the ingredients can get the chance to mix all, and the flavors can combine to create uniqueness. Taste often. Sautéed the veggies, add the broths, add the meats or beans or other main components and required spices. Taste right away. Add more salt and pepper, as you noticed it is missing. Then, usually let the soups simmer for another 20-40 minutes. Taste again. Adjust the spices. More garlic needed? No worries! Add a pinch of garlic power! More spiciness required? No worries! Add a little Sriracha, hot sauce or perhaps Tabasco sauce if you feel like it.

There is no right or wrong in the way you create or invent your next soup. Think about authenticity and yumminess meeting and creating these irresistible flavors in a bowl. That is what a soup is. It is inviting and comforting and goes well with crackers, French bread or corn chips.

If you also do not like to create a multiple course meal, opt for a soup-meal. In one bowl or portion, make sure you have your vegetables, dairy product, meat or proteins equivalents and grains. Perhaps it means you create beef and rice soup with lots of kale and tomato base. Select your favorite ingredients and make your favorite soups. It is as simple as that!

About the Author

Ivy's mission is to share her recipes with the world. Even though she is not a professional cook she has always had that flair toward cooking. Her hands create magic. She can make even the simplest recipe tastes superb. Everyone who has tried her food has astounding their compliments was what made her think about writing recipes.

She wanted everyone to have a taste of her creations aside from close family and friends. So, deciding to write recipes was her winning decision. She isn't interested in popularity, but how many people have her recipes reached and touched people. Each recipe in her cookbooks is special and has a special meaning in her life. This means that each recipe is created with attention and love. Every ingredient carefully picked, every combination tried and tested.

Her mission started on her birthday about 9 years ago, when her guests couldn't stop prizing the food on the table. The next thing she did was organizing an event where chefs from restaurants were tasting her recipes. This event gave her the courage to start spreading her recipes.

She has written many cookbooks and she is still working on more. There is no end in the art of cooking; all you need is inspiration, love, and dedication.

Author's Afterthoughts

I am thankful for downloading this book and taking the time to read it. I know that you have learned a lot and you had a great time reading it. Writing books is the best way to share the skills I have with your and the best tips too.

I know that there are many books and choosing my book is amazing. I am thankful that you stopped and took time to decide. You made a great decision and I am sure that you enjoyed it.

I will be even happier if you provide honest feedback about my book. Feedbacks helped by growing and they still do. They help me to choose better content and new ideas. So, maybe your feedback can trigger an idea for my next book.

Thank you again

Sincerely

Ivy Hope

Made in United States
Orlando, FL
13 March 2025

59427324R00037